Make It Last:
Ensuring Your Nest Egg is Around as Long as You Are

MakeItLastBook.com

Victor J. Medina, Esq.
Medina Law Group
Private Client Capital Group

ISBN-13: 978-1523977345
ISBN-10: 1523977345

Cover Image/design by – SmartMarketing, Inc.

Medina Law Group
Private Client Capital Group

65 S. Main St.
Pennington, NJ 08534
(609) 818-0068
MedinaLawGroup.com
PrivateClientCapitalGroup.com

Acknowledgements

I want to thank my family, first, for their support and understanding throughout the writing of this book.

Specifically, I want to thank my wife, Jennifer, for her love, patience and support. I also want to thank my children for their understanding as I steal time away from being with them to complete this project.

My parents, all four of them, deserve a tremendous thank you for all of their support and guidance through the years. I love you all very much.

My professional practice has benefited by the mentorship of generous advisors who have given selflessly over the years. I want to thank Mark Merenda and Steve Riley specifically for their tutelage and friendship.

I am fortunate to have colleagues who have provided ideas, laughs, and encouragement to continue. To my lawyer friends, Mark Metzger, Neel Shah, Anna Byrne, Gary Garland, Garin Muranaka, and Jason Bundick – thanks.

My ideas and visions are turned into reality by Julianna Maria, who I was fortunate to befriend, have as a client, and now have helping me work towards building something extraordinary. I am thankful for your loyalty and support.

Finally, my clients have provided this book's purpose and inspiration. It is in service to them that any of this exists. It is an honor to be your trusted counsel, and I thank you.

Dedicated to my wife Jennifer,
and my boys, Aidan, Lucas, and Dylan

Disclaimers & Terms of Use

BY CONSULTING THIS GUIDE BOOK ALL USERS UNDERSTAND, ACKNOWLEDGE, AND AGREE TO ALL OF THE FOLLOWING DISCLAIMERS AND TERMS OF USE:

THIS PUBLICATION IS FOR INFORMATIONAL PURPOSES ONLY. NONE OF THE GENERAL LEGAL AND FINANCIAL TOPICS DISCUSSED IN THIS PUBLICATION ARE TO BE CONSTRUED AS LEGAL OR FINANCIAL/ INVESTMENT ADVICE AND SHOULD NOT BE REGARDED AS SUCH. THIS BOOK IS NOT DESIGNED TO REPLACE ANY LEGAL ADVICE BY LICENSED AND QUALIFIED LEGAL ADVISORS OR FINANCIAL/ INVESTMENT ADVICE BY LICENSED AND QUALIFIED FINANCIAL/ INVESTMENT ADVISORS.

THIS IS AN EDUCATIONAL PUBLICATION DESIGNED TO EDUCATE USERS ABOUT LEGAL AND FINANCIAL TOPICS AND ISSUES THAT IMPACT INDIVIDUALS IN GENERAL. THESE ISSUES MAY OR MAY NOT AFFECT ANY INDIVIDUALS AND IF SO MAY AFFECT INDIVIDUALS DIFFERENTLY. THE TOPICS DISCUSSED IN THIS PUBLICATION ARE PROVIDED TO FACILITATE YOUR EDUCATED AND INFORMED DISCUSSIONS WITH YOUR TRUSTED LEGAL AND FINANCIAL/ INVESTMENT ADVISORS.

THE INFORMATION CONTAINED IN THIS PUBLICATION IS BELIEVED TO BE ACCURATE. HOWEVER, LAWS, CIRCUMSTANCES, AND SEVERAL OTHER UNKNOWN FACTORS CAN RENDER ANY CONTENT CONTAINED HEREIN TO BE UNRELIABLE, UNUSABLE, AND/OR INACCURATE AT ANY TIME AND WITHOUT NOTIFICATION. ALL USERS ASSUME FULL RESPONSIBILITY FOR OUTCOMES AND RESULTS FROM APPLICATION OF OR RELIANCE ON THIS MATERIAL.

ALL USERS ACCEPT FULL RESPONSIBILITY FOR CONSULTING QUALIFIED LEGAL AND/OR FINANCIAL COUNSEL TO DISCUSS THIS MATERIAL AND THEIR OWN UNIQUE LEGAL AND/OR FINANCIAL CONCERNS, ISSUES, AND CIRCUMSTANCES. THE AUTHOR, PUBLISHER, AND ANY AFFILIATES MAKE NO OFFERS, PROMISES, WARRANTIES, OR GUARANTEES OF ANY TYPE TO ANYONE BY ALLOWING ACCESS TO THIS PUBLICATION.

Table of Contents

How To Read This Book

This book is meant to be read from start to finish. Weird, right? What I mean is, I'm building a foundation for you to be able to evaluate whether you have the right plan to take you through retirement. I have distilled my advice into 10 chapters, which will lead to 5 essential elements of a "Make It Last" plan.

To help you along the way, there are three tools I have included with this book.

Tool 1: Resources at http://www.makeitlastbook.com/tools – these are downloads and templates that I use in my practice that I'm giving to you. You'll see what they are and where they belong in the chapters ahead.

Tool 2: Glossary of Terms. Too often the financial world is talking past you with words and phrases that make no sense. The glossary at the end of this book gives you no-jargon definitions of commonly-used phrases. If you want to know what words make the cut as "needing to be in a glossary", ask my parents.

Tool 3: Essential Elements of a "Make It Last" Plan Checklist. When you're done with the book, this is the checklist you should use to see whether you have a Make It Last plan or not. You can skip ahead and look at it now, but I don't recommend it. Read the book first.

1 – The Story of Paul & Diane, or Why This Guide Exists

For over a decade now, I have been helping families protect and preserve their assets. Along the way, my work has guided families through the elaborate maze of estate planning, financial retirement planning, eldercare planning, long-term care planning, income tax planning, estate tax planning, and estate administration. And with each new client, I am reminded of why I am so passionate about the work that I do and the clients I serve.

Preparing for one's retirement and legacy is important work. I take great pride in helping families put plans in place to navigate the rest of their days, and take care of their loved ones after they are gone. Mistakes in estate and financial planning can have a devastating impact on a family, which can go on to affect generations to come. For that reason, my team and I are committed to helping our clients understand the numerous elements **critical** to a well-planned estate and a smooth retirement, and then implementing that plan as their trusted advisor.

Sometimes, though despite our best guidance and advice, it is possible for a client to be misdirected by others with a conflicting agenda, or limited expertise. This can easily occur when a "financial professional" who is actually a salesperson dressed in an advisor's clothing — with a quota to fill — interferes with the plan, or fakes competence in a critical area.

And when the alternative advice shifts my client's plan out of alignment with their goals and intentions, especially in estate planning, the results are devastating since we don't find out about the error until it's too late to do anything about it. My hope is that by sharing several important insights with you, through this book, you will not experience what happened to my clients, Paul and Diane.

Paul and Diane (*names have been changed to protect clients' identities*) had come in to see me about estate planning, specifically some long-term care planning to help protect their assets should one of them become sick and need a nursing home or assisted living facility. We created a great plan for them, complete with documents that would build stone castles around their money to protect them from going broke in a nursing home. However, the success of the plan hinged on making sure that their assets were transferred into the customized trust that we had prepared for them. One of those assets was their home, which we transferred into their trust as an extension of our legal work, as they signed the rest of their papers.

The next step for Paul and Diane was to meet with their financial "professional" to arrange to have their investment and retirement assets moved into the trust. However, rather than follow through with the very carefully-structured estate plan and asset transfers that we laid out for them, the investment salesperson suggested a financial product that paid him a generous commission. Despite being a "suitable" investment — which was the only regulatory protection in place — it was not in their best interests. Worse still, it cut the legs out from under their protection plan, and the results were devastating.

Paul and Diane went forward with this financial product without consulting me, and we didn't hear from them again until Diane got sick with a form of dementia. When Paul called me, Diane was going to be moving into an assisted living facility because she was a wander risk.

It was time to trigger the asset protection element of the plan, but when I reviewed their assets, I was shocked to see that the principal place where they put their money was in a variable annuity, owned by Diane.

Now, I had been clear that they shouldn't consider any annuity owned by them individually, and specifically that they should stay away from variable annuities. But, their financial advisor, who was "such a nice guy," whom they had known "for years," had talked them into this product that likely paid a commission north of 9% and locked up their money for 20 years. Their "trusted advisor" had sold them on the concept of a premium bonus and income rider. And Paul was certain that his money had grown 13.5% since the time they bought it.

It's not helpful to get lost in the specifics about why they didn't have what they thought they had — there's a whole chapter on that! Let's just say that the numbers they were looking at were a false set of numbers and their actual principal (because the variable annuity was participating in the market and the market had been down) had shrunk by 20%. To make matters worse, there were compounding income tax and surrender charge issues, limiting how much money was actually available for them to spend or save.

In the end, Medicaid forced them to spend another half before they could qualify for benefits, and Paul was left with $23k in his name by the time Medicaid took over paying for Diane's care (Diane had almost nothing). The only asset they had protected was their home, which Paul had to sell to have any kind of money for his day-to-day expenses. And the worst part is that this result was totally avoidable if they had received the proper financial advice in the beginning.

I wish I could say that what happened to Paul and Diane was a rare event. Unfortunately, it is not.

I've seen people given no advice or bad tax advice that has caused widows to wonder where $500 a month had gone the month after their husbands died (**See Chapter 5** on income taxes for more on this). Time and time again I've seen financial advice misaligned with what the client needed, and not at all integrated with their overall plan.

Sometimes it was because their "financial professional" was greedy.

Sometimes, the advisor tried as hard as they knew, and they were well-meaning, but they didn't have the skill set to guide them through retirement. They were a decent guide, but they didn't know how to get through that jungle, and it ended up costing my client real money.

My hope is that this book will help you to navigate through some of the biggest risks to the success of your estate planning and retirement. I believe that the relationship between an attorney and a client is a sacred partnership – which is why I make an overwhelming commitment to the well-being of my clients. It is this commitment that has compelled me to prepare this important guide to help you to determine the safest course of action — to be certain that your needs, and your family's needs, are secured by the perfect plan for you.

2 – Figuring Out What You Have and What You'll Need

Although every family's financial planning process and objectives are unique and individualized, there are some elements that are standard and necessary for everyone who wishes to establish a solid plan. Just as in any journey, you need to know where you are and where you want to go before you can ever hope to establish an effective path to get there. Otherwise, it's no better than being dropped in the middle of the woods, and you start walking "that way" because it "looks good."

Step One in this process requires that you take a full inventory. You need to clarify and determine your assets, liabilities, net worth, income, expenses, cash flow, any anticipated changes in any of these, and any anticipated special needs or obligations.

(Now, if you consider this stuff basic, and you know it already, don't lose interest and stop reading the book. We are going to hit the more advanced topics in a bit, but realize that most people don't have the basics down and need to go through these steps. You may even learn something by trying our recommended approach.)

By taking inventory, you will be able to determine your actual net worth. Your Net Worth is simply all of your assets minus all of your liabilities. However, for many, determining this can be easier said than done.

Even in my own family, this has been a bit of a challenge. I remember when I began helping my father to take inventory, he kept discovering various accounts that he had forgotten he owned. He had been planning for his winter retirement for so long, yet it took a week to find all the little acorns he'd been burying for most of his working life. The shocking part was that, added together, these forgotten assets made up almost 40% of his retirement money. Even more shocking is that this is a very common experience.

Many families have discovered that they may have opened an account in the past that is now inactive, even though assets remain in the account. Over time, these accounts grow in value, albeit slowly and passively, but they accrue nonetheless. So your first challenge is to "find the money" — all of it.

I'll give a tip about how we do it in our office for clients: start with a simple spreadsheet. You can use Microsoft Excel, Apple's free Numbers program, or even Google's Sheets (which is also free and online, but limit the personal data that you put on there).

Break your assets down into the following categories:

- Real Property Assets
    - Your primary residence, any pieds-à-terre, rental properties, vacation properties, and any time-share interests.

- Cash/Cash Equivalents
    - This includes cash, checking, savings, money market accounts, certificates of deposit, etc.

- Brokerage/Investment Accounts
    - This includes all brokerage and other investment account assets, stocks, bonds, mutual funds, units in investment trusts (such as real estate investment trusts or REITs), precious metals, coins, etc.

- Tax-Deferred Retirement Accounts (401k/IRA)
    - This includes any assets in IRAs, Rollovers, SEPs, 401(k)s, 403(b)s, etc.

- Annuities (Qualified/Non-Qualified)
    - *These include any annuities that you have purchased, either inside or outside of a retirement account. Because of their unique nature, annuities should be listed separately.*

- Insurance Assets
    - *This is the cash value of any life insurance policies, long-term care insurance, group life policies, but NOT any annuities.*

- Business Interests
    - *This could include any businesses you own, have an interest in, or have invested in. This could also include the value of intellectual property, royalties due, trademarks, copyrights, patents, etc.*

- Personal Property
    - *This includes assets that are used or experienced and not necessarily easily liquidated or appraised. This includes art, jewelry, firearms, furs, boats, autos, etc.*

- Miscellaneous
    - *This could include stock options (clarify all vesting schedules and amounts), other deferred compensation, accounts receivables, money owed to you, and anything else that you own or to which you have rights.*

From there you will have to write down information such as:

- Account Value
- Account Number
- Account Holder (this is you, or your spouse, etc.)
- Financial Institution
- Tax Basis (if known)
- Notes (for contract terms, limitations, easements, etc.)

To help you, I have included a free template you can use to start. Go to **www.MakeItLastBook.com/tools**.

It could be you may know where to find most of this stuff, but if you want to avoid what my dad did, there are some tips to finding forgotten assets. Start with your most recent tax return. Chances are you may have bundled all of your tax statements and 1099s and delivered them to your tax preparer, without scrutinizing them. Most likely these 1099s are stapled to your filed paperwork. Start here.

Next, make a list of all of the tax reporting statements you have received. This will tell you where the assets are. As I mentioned, we organize a client's assets in this way when we help with legal or financial planning. It is highly beneficial to have a trusted advisor to guide you through this inventory process because many times the information you need isn't something plainly listed on the account statements. An experienced estate and financial planning advisor can help you to properly categorize each of your assets and liabilities.

Now that you have totaled up what you own, you have earned the right to do a "happy dance." However, only a short one because it's now time to add up what you owe to others. You need to itemize every penny that you owe. These are called your liabilities.

Liabilities:

These could include:

- Mortgages
- Lines of Credit
- Auto Loans
- Personal loans
- Investment account loans
- Loans against any of your assets

- Any accounts payable
- Plus, any other debts, liens, or financial obligations you have.

Again, our template will help you capture most of these, but you could also use any of the financial planning tools available to the public, such as QuickBooks, or new online programs like Mint.

Once you know your total assets and your total liabilities you can calculate the net difference, which is your net worth.

Cash Flow

Next you need to assess your current cash flow and your expected changes in cash flow vs. needs. Itemize all sources of income and inflows of assets. Again, a trusted advisor can help you to properly evaluate and assess each inflow source. Similar to determining your net worth, you need to determine the net of your inflows (income, interest, assets procured) vs. your outflows (all of your bills and liability repayments). Another important piece of information to collect is the tax category for the assets, such as "ordinary income tax," "capital gains," "qualified dividends," etc.

At this point you should have a really clear picture of where you are financially. Now the big question is, what's next?

Well, actually, it's a series of additional big questions such as:

- What do you want to change or stay the same?

- How will your income change as you approach retirement?

- If you are already retired, what changes do you anticipate in your resources? How will your needs change?

- Do you have enough assets to generate the income you will need for the rest of your life (and your spouse's life)?

- How much do you want protected? How much can be affected by the volatility of the market?

- What do you want to provide for your family and the next generations?

Here also, you should be walking through a series of questions, like:

- What are your goals?

- What additional family challenges or needs will shape your estate plan?

- Do you plan to liquidate or consolidate your assets?

- Do you plan extensive travel?

- Do you want to help fund your grandchildren's education?

- Do you have a special needs child that you need to provide for?

- Do you need to prepare for long-term care protection?

- Do you want to make sure that your grandchildren receive an inheritance that bypasses your children or a daughter or son-in-law?

- Is there anything else that you want to make sure is protected for you, your spouse, and your family?

You will need to determine how much your income is going to change and if it is still adequate to support your anticipated lifestyle. If not, you may need to evaluate your expenses to decide what stays and what goes. By clarifying your income and your expenses, you could find yourself at the challenging crossroads of change.

There's no mistaking that this work can be boring, tedious, and may even be a little depressing as you reach conclusions about what you have, what you owe, and what you need. Despite the challenge of this process, it cannot be skipped or completed hastily. It is a vital step.

If you fail to do this foundational work correctly and completely, then all of your preparation will be inaccurate and even worse, inadequate. You'll be back to being "dropped in the woods" and guessing about where you're going and how to get there.

The easiest way to assure that you are being accurate and thorough is to have a specialist to assist you with properly itemizing and categorizing your estate, in addition to helping you map-out an effective plan to protect your assets, access the income you will need with minimal tax exposure, and preserve your estate value for your heirs.

Last tip: I know that these insights can be emotionally draining. However, I want you to know that there are more exciting and uplifting elements to estate and financial planning (in upcoming chapters). There will be solutions to guide you through your problems, and ways of getting you comfortable and optimistic about your future. It is what you do now, that will help you to make sure you'll be able to do what you want to do, for the rest of your life.

3 – Why Your Investment Strategy Needs to Change in Retirement, or *Why You May Not Be Able to Dance with the One that "Brung Ya"*

As you approach retirement (or even now as you are *in* retirement), the most important realization you may make is that the investment strategy that has served you thus far, may no longer serve your needs. The reality is that in post-retirement you will be presented with a different arena of risks that must be mitigated to protect your estate, preserve your livelihood, and maintain your quality of life. And in order to mitigate the variety of new risks that most retirees face, there will likely be a need to make adjustments to how you invest, and what you invest in.

During your working years and wealth accumulation phase, you may have had an investment strategy that was patient, passive, and selective. You may have selected an "aggressive" investment approach, with lots of ups and downs to the roller coaster, because you could afford to wait for appreciation or recovery during market dips. In addition, your cash flow likely wasn't affected by this volatility because you had a regular paycheck coming in from work.

In fact, this more aggressive approach is generally a very prudent wealth accumulation strategy. You may have also tolerated even most aggressive, short-term investments with higher risk and greater return potential because your need for those assets wasn't in the near term, and if you suffered a catastrophic loss of those assets...well, you had time to make it up, understanding that no results are guaranteed.

Neither one of these investment philosophies will serve you well in retirement. During retirement, you need more certainty and better preservation of your assets. All risks must be evaluated for how they will serve you or potentially harm you in the post-retirement phase of your financial planning. Some investors who shied away from any form of guaranteed income may want to think about that now to help supplement social security and pension income (assuming you have any).

Some may presume that if "buy-and-hold" equity investments and aggressive higher risk investments are ill-advised during retirement because of volatility risks, then a portfolio with a majority bond mix must be the best alternative.

You ready for a real head trip? A portfolio with mostly bonds could also be ill-advised during retirement.

Bonds have characteristics that could jeopardize your asset preservation. They are directly impacted by unpredictable fluctuations in interest rates and may fail to keep pace with inflation. Said another way, even though bonds may be "safer," their interest-rate sensitivity could have you losing pace with the pack as your money buys less and less over time.

For the investor with sufficient investable assets, you may be better served with an investment approach that separates your assets into long, mid, and short-term segments with distinct investments and strategies for each segment.

Generally, what I do for my clients is to help them organize their post-retirement assets into hypothetical "buckets." Each bucket represents the purpose of the asset cluster. It could be a short-term, mid-term, or long-term investment bucket. Then I help my clients to define a specific investment strategy for each bucket of assets.

While results are never guaranteed, each bucket, or asset cluster, is managed in a way that shields the assets from risk exposures that would cause serious jeopardy to the underlying assets, while pursuing a focus that is in tandem with the time frame and risk tolerance for that portion of the overall portfolio.

Sequence of Returns Risk

Regardless of the bucket category, one of the biggest challenges to all retirees is managing their sequence-of-returns risk. Many early retirees have never heard of the concept of sequence of returns, despite its potential to have a devastating impact on one's ability to preserve sustainable retirement income. Even worse, many investment sales representatives, posing as financial planners, aren't aware of sequence-of-returns risk either. The simple explanation is that sequence-of-returns risk is the risk of mistiming the market when you need money.

"Observe due measure, for right timing
is in all things the most important factor."
− Hesiod (Greek Poet approx. 700 BC)

In other words, timing is everything. So what does sequence of returns and timing have to do with your asset preservation strategy?

In short, the answer is a lot.

Here is how sequence-of-returns risk can affect your retirement nest egg:

Let's assume you have a $1,000,000 nest egg. I'm choosing $1,000,000 because it's a round number that makes the math here easier. Your nest egg could be bigger or smaller.

Hypothetically, let's also assume that you need $50,000 income per year to make ends meet. Now, for this discussion, any returns are for purposes of illustration only. No return is ever guaranteed.

- In Year 1, you pull $50,000 out of your nest egg,
  - leaving $950,000 to grow at, let's say, 2%
  - and, that nest egg will only grow to $969,000.

- Then in Year 2, you take out another $50,000,
  - leaving only $919,000 to earn another 2%
  - so then, that nest egg will only grow to $937,380

- Then in Year 3, you take out another $50,000,
  - leaving only $887,380 to earn another 2%
  - that nest egg will only grow to $905,128

So by Year 4, before you pull your next deduction, you will have already depleted almost 10% of your nest egg.

This pattern could have a devastating effect on your ability to ensure that your nest egg is around as long as you are, especially if your money doesn't grow…but instead goes *down* in a given year.

Remember, it takes more growth to make up a loss than the loss itself. If you lose 20% of $100, you'll be down to $80. If you then gained 20% on that money the next year, you'd only be at $96. Imagine compounding that problem with taking principal out of what you have.

Said another way, if you start to deduct from your retirement nest egg when the market is in a downturn and interest rates are low, your sequence-of-returns risk is higher and your nest egg will deplete much more quickly. This is very important to understand as you plan for your retirement. As illustrated, the impact could be quite significant.

While this does not mean you shouldn't retire or access your nest egg at all if the market is doing poorly when you want to retire, it does mean you need to plan for this possibility and make adjustments in your investment strategy to minimize its impact. This is where an experienced retirement distribution planning specialist can help to guide you to the best solutions for you and your family.

So, given that you have no control over the equity markets, interest rates, or the cost-of-living increases, how can you sail a steady ship amid a sea of uncertainty? The answer is with regular comprehensive financial planning and with the help of someone who focuses exclusively in estate planning and asset preservation.

As an aside, I know that a hallmark of the financial planning profession is using software to create 200-page tombstone financial plans. These plans are impressive and imposing. They are filled with lots of boilerplate – so much so, that you wonder if the software programmers were getting paid by the word. In any event, the problem is that by the time the plan is done printing, it's outdated.

I much prefer my approach, which is to create a 1-page financial plan with no more than 3-5 action items. This plan is then reviewed and updated annually. It's far easier to make small course corrections with a nimble speedboat than it is to set off in an aircraft carrier and try to change directions after you've gotten miles off course.

Back to the actual investment advice. When I begin work with clients, sometimes the first challenge is to purge any misguided investment habits that can wreak havoc on one's assets. Sound financial planning focuses on the elements that you can control, instead of making investments based on sensational headlines in the media, "hot tips," "inside scoops," emotions, impulse, and predictions.

These are all factors, known to cause harm to an estate's value. And I'm facing an uphill battle since the financial media, and even the national media, has time to fill and advertising to sell. They'll never run out of ways to get you excited about what you should be doing with your money. And there's no accountability for yesterday's advice, because there's another 7-minute segment to fill today and tomorrow.

For clients who are at or approaching retirement, your best defense against outliving your resources (nest egg) is to establish a comprehensive financial and investment plan (that addresses *your* priorities and needs) with elements to mitigate any risks that you specifically expect to encounter.

The best plans focus on scientific and historical patterns and expectations, reduced volatility, reduced expenses and asset turnover, asset class diversification, and consistent discipline.

When someone outlives their estate, you can usually trace the root cause back to a breakdown in one of these core focal points.

4 – How to Avoid Dying Broke in a Nursing Home

One of the most overlooked risks to a family's estate is the potential impact of chronic illness, disability, and the need for assisted living or extended nursing care. The reasons are obvious. Who really wants to think about the possibility that they will one day be unable to take care of their own basic needs? And who wants to think about what assets they have to give up just to qualify for government assistance with elder care expenses?

However, my goal is to help you to look at this challenging situation in a whole new way. I want to make sure you have the facts and some solutions so that you can confidently address this risk from an empowered position. Instead of avoiding the issue — and inviting financial disaster — I will show you how to confront the issue and secure asset preserving solutions.

It is first important that you understand the specialty of elder care law. The role of an elder care law specialist is to make sure that you are adequately prepared for the financial, medical, and legal challenges that you will face as you grow older. This generally involves a variety of issues that must be addressed such as: disability and long-term care planning, Medicaid planning, veteran's benefits, health care directives, powers of attorney, guardianships, and foundational estate planning. The objective is to secure maximum protection of your assets along with funding for any assisted living or nursing care if that becomes necessary.

First the bad news:

On average, 1 in every 2 women and 1 in every 4 men will require some degree of living assistance or nursing care at some point in their lives. Guys, before you do that "happy dance" again, the reason women are twice as likely to need long-term care is because they live longer. In other words, you're going die sooner — stop dancing.

More bad news:

The cost of long-term care, such as assisted living or nursing homes, is mind-numbingly staggering. On average, monthly nursing home care costs can be around $9,000...every month. That means that just 1 year in a facility, could cost your family over $100,000, and you may be there for more than one year. And that's just for 1 person. What if both you and your spouse needed assisted care? What would happen to your life savings?

While the likelihood you will need long-term-care is some percentage between 25-50%, the effect of needing long-term care is going to be felt at either 0% or 100%. There is no middle ground. What you need to be considering is whether you are going to take your chances, and risk being on the wrong side of a guess that starts penalizing you at a rate of $9,000/month or more. And, given the rapidly increasing cost of care, it's very likely that that number will rise very quickly.

Now for some myth busting:

One huge problem in elder care issues is the amount of inaccurate information that is spread by people, who may have good intentions, but not the facts. This is particularly the case when it comes to qualifying for Medicaid assistance to help with long-term care expenses. The most common misconception is that in order to meet the financial test to qualify for Medicaid, you need to give away all of your assets, be broke, or lose your home. This is not the case. (In fact, giving away assets at the wrong time or in the wrong way can have devastating consequences as you'll read in a second.)

I focus my legal practice in elder care law, so I know of dozens of ways to help you legally preserve the maximum amount of assets and income and still qualify for Medicaid benefits, in the shortest amount of time, even mid-crisis. So first things first, do not let well-intentioned but misinformed friends, co- workers, family, and any other "know-it-alls" give you highly-specialized legal advice.

The most important thing to understand is that a mistake here could cost you tens and tens of thousands of dollars and months of eligibility for Medicaid and other benefits. Given the high cost of long-term care, these mistakes could easily leave the remaining spouse without sufficient resources to maintain their quality of life, or put them behind a very large 8-ball for the rest of their days.

Here is where experienced elder care legal advice can help you to preserve your nest egg and avoid penalties or challenges to benefits.

What about long-term care insurance?

I'm glad you asked. Well, long-term care insurance is kind of like a double-edged sword. First the good side: long-term care insurance is an insurance product specifically designed to address the expense of extended care in a community program, home health care, or in a skilled services facility.

Now the bad side:

- Long-term care (LTC) insurance, similar to life insurance, is more expensive the older you are when you start a policy. But unlike death, which everyone must deal with at some point, long-term care insurance may only be needed by half of those in retirement. So there's an approximately 50% chance your premiums will be wasted.

- About those premiums...well that's where you'll really feel the edge of that sword. LTC insurance premiums have been rising at an alarming and cost prohibitive rate. The families who need LTC insurance the most, probably can't afford it. And the insurance companies can and will increase premiums as you get older while the risk of you getting sick (and needing the policy) increases. So, for retirees on a fixed income, their cash flow could be impacted to a level that causes them to drop the policy just when they may need it most.

- Underwriting is challenging. Basically, the more it looks like you need it or the longer you wait to get it, the more likely the premiums will be unaffordable.

Despite the challenge of meeting the significant cost of potential long-term care needs, the insurance industry continues to evolve to meet the demand with innovative and consumer-driven solutions. One potential solution is a "hybrid" policy. These are life insurance or annuity policies with long-term care benefits.

Here's how a Hybrid Policy works:

- First you can choose a single-premium or short-pay premium so that the policy is paid-up, quickly. This protects you from a policy lapsing. You can "set it and forget it," until you need it.

- You can choose a policy with a guaranteed return-of-premium (something that is not available with straight long-term care insurance), so that at a minimum your policy will pay out all of the premiums you paid in.

- Your policy could have a guaranteed death benefit (income tax-free asset transfer to your heirs).

- One policy can provide coverage for each spouse with benefits available for both.

- Here's the best part: with a long-term care, disability, or chronic illness rider you can receive an advance/accelerated access to your death benefit to cover specific long-term care related expenses. So if you need it – you've got it! If you don't need it, the full death benefit transfers to your heirs.

- You have flexibility in how funds are used (for example, you could use your accelerated benefit to pay a grandchild to live with you and be your caregiver rather than pay a nursing home).

- Now, if you are in the group that never requires LTC – your money won't be wasted. Your entire death benefit will be paid income tax-free to your heirs.

- If you only need a short amount of nursing care, then you can access only what you need from your accelerated benefit and leave the rest to maintain more death benefit.

- If you need substantial LTC, then you can use your full accelerated benefit to pay for your LTC expenses, while still maintaining a guaranteed death benefit.

- This can easily be a perfect alternative to assets that offer very little income and no benefits at all, like certificates of deposit.

This is the retirement and financial planning equivalent to "the best of both worlds" or "have your cake and eat it too!"

Haven't heard of this type of policy before? Not a surprise. If you have been primarily working with investment sales people and insurance sales reps rather than an experienced financial planner, you may only be offered the products that each salesperson has to sell vs. the perfect tool to meet your exact financial and estate needs (See Chapter 6 about Proprietary Assets). Here is where an experienced, and independent, elder law advisor is critical to your planning process.

One last thought: If for any reason you were unable to attend to your affairs, who should make decisions on your behalf? And are there any important medical directives that you would prefer to be followed on your behalf? Whatever your preferences are, they must be in writing if you wish for them to be known and honored.

The reason this legal advice is making its way into a financial discussion is that the failure to have proper paperwork in place can lead to the need for a guardianship. In my neck of the woods, that will run you between $5,000 and $7,500 for a simple uncontested guardianship.

It's not enough just to have power of attorney papers. You need to know whether they'll work when you need them to – which means you should be "field testing" them before you become incapacitated — because if you wait until then, well, it's too late to get new ones drawn up.

5 – Income Taxes in Retirement: The Monster Stealing Your Socks at Night

A few years ago Doris (*again, not her real name*) came to meet with me about updating her estate planning. Her husband had recently passed away and she needed to update her documents to remove his name and make some other changes.

As part of my regular interview, we began to talk about finances. Sometimes the first spouse to go is the financially savvy spouse, and that can be a rude awakening. That wasn't Doris' situation – she was always right on top of the finances, but she said something in passing that caused my ears to perk up. She mentioned that ever since her husband died, she had less money to spend. She owed more in taxes the next April, and she couldn't understand why. From her vantage point, everything looked like it stayed the same, and her expenses were down with only one of them still around.

As I looked into it a bit, I discovered that what was causing her to have less money in her pocket had to do with her filing status. She was now "single" and there are different tax rates for single people versus filing as "married."

Of course, there wasn't much she could do about that situation now. But, Doris and her husband had a sizable IRA.

As you'll learn in a bit, there was a lot they could have done to save on income taxes if they had taken some steps while both of them were alive.

What I learned from working with Doris is that income taxation is something that retirees (and pre-retirees) need to focus on early in the process. Proactive income tax planning even impacts the discussion about when to take Social Security.

In this chapter, you'll learn some of the techniques to reduce income taxes — techniques that I use with clients every year. What's important here, though, is that income tax planning is a **proactive** set of activities.

The problem with most income tax planning in retirement is that it comes the next April, after it's too late to do anything about it. Advisors should be doing better than that.

Good income tax planning should start in January, as soon as the federal government releases their figures for that tax year. Those numbers — the ones that set the limits for the 10%-15%-25% income tax brackets — allow you to chart a course to minimize how much the government will take out of your money. It's imperative that you focus on those numbers early in the year so you can accurately navigate the rest of the year. If you wait until December to do this planning, it's just too late.

What can you do to chart a course? I'm glad you asked. Most retirees figure that their income tax is what it is. It's the product of whatever their social security is plus their other income sources. But, there's more to it than that.

First, the amount of tax you pay on your social security is a factor of how much income you get from other sources. The more income you get from places like your IRA or ordinary interest from your bonds…the more of your social security income is included as part of your taxable income. It sounds more complicated than it really is. For purposes of income tax planning, social security is a number that messes with the calculations if you are not watching its impact.

Proactive Income Tax Planning looks at four specific tax planning strategies: Maximizing Tax Brackets, Minimizing RMD Impact, Long-Term Capital Gains Harvesting, and Inheritance Income Tax Planning.

Maximizing Tax Brackets

As I mentioned above, every year the federal government releases the income tax bracket numbers for single and married taxpayers. They give you this information ahead of time and there's nothing secret about it. Most people don't pay attention to it until the next April as they prepare their taxes. However, in retirement, those numbers are very important because of the increase in tax rate as you move from one bracket to another.

Let's use some real numbers, but remember, these are only good for 2016 (the tax year as of this writing).

Tax Rate	Single	Married
10%	$0-$9,275	$0-$18,550
15%	$9,276-$37,650	$18,551-$75,300
25%	$37,651-$91,150	$75,301-$151,900
28%	$91,151-$190,150	$151,901-$231,450

The first thing you'll notice is the jump from the second to the third tax rate. It goes from 15% to 25%. That's a marginal income tax increase of 10%! For every $100 over the 15% bracket you are, you'll be paying $10 extra in taxes. That's very significant for retirees trying to figure out if they'll have enough to get to the end.

One of the steps in our planning process is to see if clients have any more "room" in their tax bracket. If they are married and receiving $50,000 in taxable income, they are leaving $25,300 in money taxed at the 15% bracket on the table. Suppose further that they'll still receive that income after the death of one spouse, that means that $12,350 ($50,000 minus the $37,650) will be taxed at the 25% bracket. That client will be paying $1,235 more in taxes than if they had moved money out of a tax deferred account (like an IRA) before the death of the first spouse.

Another way we can work with maximizing tax brackets (or minimizing the impact of certain income) is to manage which kinds of assets are owned in which accounts. Bonds are investments that throw off interest, which is taxed at ordinary income tax rates. Bonds need to be owned inside of an IRA and not in an "after-tax" account. If we can reduce the impact of bond interest on the tax profile, you can limit if you go over the 15% (for instance) with your investments.

Where you own assets (in what kind of account) is as important as the assets or investments you own.

Minimizing RMD Impact

If you have money in an IRA or 401k (or similar tax-deferred account), the federal government does not let you leave that money in there forever, and avoid paying tax on it. In fact, after you turn 70 ½ you have to start taking money out. The amount you have to take is based on your age (at 70 ½ the amount is 3.65%) and the value of the account on December 31st of the prior year. That is the "Required Minimum Distribution" or RMD.

What does this have to do with proactive income tax planning? Well, many people stop working before they turn 70 ½. That means that they are without a wage or salary income for some years. If they've been contributing to their IRA for most of their working lives, there is probably a good chunk of money in that retirement account.

While they are retired from working, and perhaps before they elect for Social Security, there is time for them to take some money out of that account (at the best tax rate) to reduce the overall value of the account before they hit 70 ½.

To illustrate this, let's use some real numbers: Let's say there is a married couple, both of whom are 62 and ready to retire. Each of them has $400,000 in an IRA, so there's $800,000 total. Let's also say that each has $25,000 in taxable income, or $50,000 total. From our chart above, we know that there is about $25,000 of room in the 15% tax bracket.

If they don't touch their IRA for the next 8 years, it's conceivable that it grows to $1,000,000 and when they turn 70½ they will have to take out about $36,500 ($1MM times 3.65%). That income will put them approximately $11,200 into the 25% bracket, causing $1,120 of marginal tax.

What if instead they took about $25,000 out of the IRA in each of the 8 years between 62 and 70 ½? Using rough numbers, they would reduce their IRA account value by about $200,000 (8 years times $25,000). That money is still invested and growing for them, but in an after-tax account, so it doesn't count as part of the 3.65% that they have to take from their IRAs. In each of the 8 years of this proactive income tax planning tactic, they've never paid more than 15% of income tax on their money. And when they reach 70 ½, there is just about $600,000 in the combined IRAs ($800,000 starting minus $200,000 of planned distributions). Their Required Minimum Distribution is just $21,900 (3.65% times $600,000).

That amount is under the 15% tax bracket limit and the couple has saved $1,120 in that year, and every year after that.

That's just a very quick example of the power of Minimizing RMD Impact. And the positive impact can be extended to planning for the early death of one spouse, where the income tax effect can be very significant as they are now filing under the "single" tax limitations.

Harvesting Capital Gains

If you check most sources, they'll tell you that the tax rate for long-term capital gains is 15%. However, that's not the entire story. In fact, long-term capital gains have three income tax rates 0%, 15%, and 20%. The rate you pay depends on how much other income you get (kind of like with Social Security).

As an example, let's use our hypothetical couple making $50,000 a year in taxable income. If you remember, the top of the 15% tax bracket is $75,300. The 0% capital gains rate would apply to the $25,300 between their taxable income and the top of the 15% bracket. In fact, any capital gains that fills the gap between their taxable income and $75,300 for a married couple or $37,650 for a single person can be realized at 0%.

Why might you want to do this? Well, think about it like hitting a reset button. You can sell and buy the same investments, and if you harvested capital gains sometime in the past, it will reduce how much capital gains you may have to pay in the future.

Let's say you have an account started at $100,000 and grew to $150,000 in 2016. There is $50,000 of long term capital gains, with a $7,500 tax bill waiting in there some time in the future. You could harvest capital gains in each of 2016 and 2017 ($25,000 a year for my hypothetical $50,000 income couple) and pay $0 in capital gains and essentially save $7,500.

Each families' circumstances are going to be very different, of course, but you can see the power of this kind of proactive income tax planning.

Inheritance Income Tax Planning

The first three income tax planning strategies are things to help retirees during their lifetime. This last strategy is one to save money in income taxes that their kids or beneficiaries would have to pay on the inheritance they are left.

To understand this kind of planning, you need to learn three principles: First, assets like homes and investment accounts with long-term capital gains get a "step-up" in basis at death. Essentially, you get to erase all of the accrued capital gains in that account at death and before the beneficiaries get the money.

Second, assets like annuities and IRA distributions are taxed at ordinary income tax rates based on who receives the income. If the retired couple withdraw money, they would pay income tax at their marginal income tax rate. But if their kids withdrew that money, they would pay income tax at that child's marginal income tax rate.

Third, assets like annuities and IRAs do not receive a basis adjustment (or step-up) at death. So their accrued gain is carried over to the next generation.

With Inheritance Income Tax Planning, I work with clients to examine their annuities and IRAs against their income tax bracket and compare that with their children's income tax brackets. Sometimes they won't know exactly what their kids (and their spouses are making), but some educated guesses show us that their kids are in a higher tax bracket than they are, if simply because the kids are still working and my clients are retired.

If that's the case, we begin to calculate how much to move out of IRAs or deferred annuities, and pay income tax at the lower rate. We can then invest that money in long-term investments that accrue capital gains. At worst, if my clients have to liquidate that money in the future, they'll pay 15% in capital gains. But, if they leave that money for their kids, the kids will escape the income tax bill (because the parent paid it) and escape the capital gains bill (because of the step-up at death).

Neat, right?

6 – How and Why You Should Steer Clear of Proprietary Assets

Whenever I begin work with a new family, our first order of business is to get a clear picture of what assets the client has, so that we can determine how to preserve the estate and secure a life-long income, (i.e. the tedious and boring stuff that we covered in **Chapter 2**). This in itself is an eye-opening experience for most, as they determine if they have enough resources to fulfill their post-retirement needs as well as any legacy wishes.

This process is always especially eye-opening whenever we discover that their portfolio includes a significant portion of proprietary assets. Many investors don't realize that they are heavily invested in proprietary assets, let alone know what those are and even more distressing – what they represent.

Before you can fully grasp the reasons for concern, it is best to clarify the distinctly different types of professions that like to call themselves "financial advisors." The best place to start is with a quick history of financial legislation.

Dating back to 1933, the Glass-Steagall Act was enacted to prohibit banks, investment firms, and insurance companies from combining operations. The belief was that this separation of financial industries along with several other provisions of the 1933 Banking Act would deliver much needed economic stability at a very challenging time.

However, after decades of wanting a piece of the business in adjacent industries (including some alleged Glass-Steagall violations such as when Citibank merged with Travelers in 1998) the financial, banking, and insurance industries got their wish.

In 1999 the Gramm-Leach-Bliley Act (GLBA) (aka the Financial Services Modernization Act of 1999) was passed to repeal the cross-industry prohibitions of the Glass-Steagall Act of 1933. What this meant was that banks, investment firms, and insurance companies could get involved in each other's business.

So what did this mean for the financial services consumer? In short a little bit of chaos and a lot of confusion. Banks started selling insurance, mutual funds, annuities, and other investment products. Insurance companies started offering bonds, certificates of deposit (CDs), savings accounts, mutual funds, and loans. And investment firms started selling insurance, money markets, CDs, savings accounts, and loans.

This "wild-west" environment produced a ton of "jacks of all trades, masters of none." Consumers became easily bombarded by a whole bunch of financial "solutions" at every turn, and everyone in the industry was calling themselves a financial advisor or wealth manager, even if they only held insurance licensed or broker's licenses to sell commissionable investments.

Now the next thing to understand is that this financial free-for-all set the stage for a surge in proprietary products. On the surface, proprietary financial products appear to be appropriate and "suitable" investments. However, they present some serious risks to the financial strength and flexibility of your portfolio. And at the heart of the issue is the way in which you acquire them and from whom.

A proprietary product is in essence a house brand. When you are offered a proprietary product you know a few important things. First, you are likely working with an investment salesperson rather than an independent financial advisor. This is a person whose main compensation is from commissions on sales of investments. Second, you may not have been offered the best solution for you, just the best one they could offer. They may appear to be the same. But they are definitely not.

Here is one way to explain the difference:

Let's assume you are in the market for a new car. You walk into a Ford dealership and you describe what you want in a car (the engine, the color, the electronic goodies). What kind of car do you think they will show you? It doesn't matter if the world of cars that serve your needs include a Ford, Honda, BMW, or Porsche. The only thing the salesperson can offer you is a Ford. They make 'em and they sell 'em. This is their proprietary product.

Here's another example:

Let's assume you go shopping for a new television. So you go to a large chain store that has its own house brand but also sells all of the main name brands. This company not only makes TVs but sells them as well. Their profit margin on their own brand is much higher if you buy the house brand vs. the name brands they offer. What you don't know is that the salesperson earns a higher commission and other perks for selling the house brand TVs instead of the other name brands. So when you ask the salesperson which one they recommend, what do you think is most likely to happen? You might get the TV that was a better deal for the salesperson, than it was for you.

These scenarios are similar to what happens when you are offered a proprietary investment product. Chances are highly likely that the "advisor" who is recommending the proprietary product is being offered some extra incentive or pressure to sell it to you. How can that ever be in your best interest? Even if the investment appears to be doing well and is considered a "suitable" match to your investment objectives and risk tolerance, how will you ever know if it really was the best option available to you?

And, there's nothing illegal about this rigged system. Your trusted salesperson isn't even obligated to tell you about this arrangement.

In addition to a potential conflict of interest and inappropriate selections (because of the advisor's nearly irresistible sales incentive), proprietary products also reduce your liquidation options and flexibility.

If you choose to move your account to another firm, you cannot take your proprietary assets with you. This means you are bound to the firm that manages that proprietary product or you will have to liquidate the assets, even if you do not want to, or if the timing is not right. In other words, they gotcha.

So what does the type of financial advisor have to do with proprietary products? A lot. Here is often where the most informed investors are defined by the type of advisor they employ, to help them manage their financial portfolio.

As I said before, there are nearly no regulations about what you call yourself if you're a financial advisor. You can call yourself financial advisor, retirement planner, wealth manager, investment professional, and the list goes on. Consumers think that the terms are interchangeable, but not all advisors are made alike.

(Even with my entity, a Registered Investment Adviser, terms can be unclear. Registration refers only to the formal process of registering with a regulatory agency, and does not indicated or imply a certain level of skill or training.)

When you are confronted with a variety of titles that financial advisors use, the first challenge is to decipher their distinctive functions, methods, incentives, and fiduciary responsibilities. Some titles may just be a fancy name for a commissioned salesperson who gets extra commission for selling proprietary products.

Generally, agents, registered representatives, and brokers, are strongly restricted in what they can offer to potential clients by their employers or "dealers." They are very likely incentivized to sell investment products pushed by their parent company as the "deal of the month," which may have absolutely nothing to do with choosing the best investments to achieve your objectives — just the best they could offer, or the best commissions being paid that month or that quarter.

This practice is pervasive across the biggest names in the industry. The names you know, the household names, the "trusted names" — they all engage in this practice as they rev up their sales people to go out and "close, close, close."

In all honesty, I didn't know much about this practice when I was just doing legal work. I found it curious that all of my clients from this one super large "investment" company held the same mutual funds. Different advisors, different life situations – same funds. It was only after I learned about proprietary assets that I came to understand why so many of these portfolios looked the same.

This practice of offering proprietary assets differs greatly from how most Registered Investment Advisers or (RIAs) conduct business. A Registered Investment Adviser, must be registered[*] with the SEC (Securities and Exchange Commission) or a state regulatory agency. They have a formal fiduciary responsibility to their clients. They are fundamentally and legally obligated to provide advice that is appropriate for the client and always act in their client's best interest.

RIAs frequently work on a fee basis rather than earning commissions based on the investment products they sell. They can generally recommend investment products that are managed by third parties rather than their "employer," and as independents, can draw from the entire universe of investments — selecting only those that are best for each client.

---

[*] **Registration refers only to the formal process of registering with a regulatory agency, and does not indicate or imply a certain level of skill or training.**

RIAs are more likely to function as independents with complete responsibility to helping their clients select the best options to match their investment needs and risk tolerance. And their fees can be tied to the amount of assets they are entrusted with rather than the amount of transactions they recommend — which means that your financial futures are tied together.

When you make more money — so do they. When you make less money — so do they.

Quite a different world from advisors that make their money on commission, whether or not their recommendations are what you really need.

In summary, proprietary assets present a variety of disadvantages that can restrict your portfolio's flexibility. They may also have been recommended by a "financial advisor" who received extra incentives to convince you that their "house brand" was the right choice over the best choices among third party options. And they are often an indicator that you are working with an advisor who might be making recommendations based more on what's in his best interest than yours.

7 – Turning Off the Leaky Faucet: The Impact of Hidden Fees and How to Avoid Them

There is another key area of insight that is critical for investors, especially retirees, to know and manage. You *must know* all of the fees (declared and hidden) that are associated with each of your investments. This is where you can discover that a no-load mutual fund (one that charges no commission to purchase it) might actually be loaded with hidden fees.

Hidden fees really are like a "leaky faucet" in your portfolio. They represent fees that covertly deplete the assets in your estate. And just like with a "leaky faucet" they could become quite costly, one drip at a time. The key is to discover them, and move to lower-cost alternatives, so that you can streamline your portfolio.

Some of the biggest culprits in the hidden fee arena are mutual funds. Even when an investment touts a no-load structure, there could be a significant amount of hidden fees already built into the investment.

Some of the fees associated with mutual funds include:

Sales loads: These are the commission fees paid to the sales rep and the firm that sold the investment product. Some funds are advertised as "no-load". Yet, even a no-load fund can generate significant hidden fee revenue for the fund managers and sales reps — it may not be in the form of a "sales load" and may be some of the 12b-1 fees discussed below.

Transaction/Trading fees: When a security is bought or sold inside the fund portfolio, there could be a transaction fee assessed against the fund assets.

Fund fees: This is like a regular and ongoing administration fee, that is charged against the fund's assets on a quarterly basis.

Mutual funds use the term "expense ratio" to describe various operational costs that are charged against the fund's assets. This consolidated expense includes an interesting variety of fees that the fund manager charges the fund, for performing the role of fund manager. There are sometimes multiple layers of fees, some which are undisclosed, such as 12b-1 fees, to cover distribution costs and sales expenses. If you recall the discussion of proprietary investment vehicles, you can see how some investment firms not only sell investment products but also like to create the products that their sales reps will be selling and recommending. This can be a very lucrative operation.

The expense ratio fee often includes charges for administering the fund, record-keeping, compliance costs, and other operational costs. However, the real insult is that it also includes charges for marketing costs, shareholder services, and distribution costs. In other words, you're paying for them to advertise the fund, for them to service your account, and for them to sell it to you.

Even if the fund advertises that they are no-load and charge no upfront commission, they actually are charging you a fee for selling it to you, not just once, but *every year*. In fact, one of the dirty little secrets in the investment brokerage world is that some financial sales reps make pretty good livings from the quarterly bonuses they earn for having millions of client dollars invested in no-load funds. Guess who's paying for those quarterly bonuses.

The expense ratio is usually hard, but not impossible to find. It should be stated in the fund prospectus and on the fund manager website. Some major investment newspapers will also publish mutual fund expense ratios.

Now, one other aspect of these hidden fees is that they are sometimes declared in a manner that downplays their significance and impact. After all, how bad could an expense ratio of let's say just 2% be? You would be surprised.

First you need to understand how the expense ratio fee is paid to the fund manager. Let's assume that a fund has a good year and grows by 10%. If the fund has a 2% annual fee, that 10% return becomes only 8% for investors, after the expense ratio is charged against the fund's value. But what if the fund breaks even for the year? The fund manager is still going to charge the fund that 2% management expense fee. So that means that even when the fund breaks even, investors will still lose 2% in value. So you can see that you pay for it one way or another – every year.

This 2% fee example just illustrates the impact in a single year. Now let's look at the impact over time. One of the calculations that I have done for clients is a comparison of the impact of 2 different fees: 1.44% (which is an average for mutual funds) and 0.33% (which is typical for the portfolios we recommend). For this comparison I used the following same controls:

- Starting Investment $10,000
- Impact assessed after 10 years
- Assuming an average annual return of 7% (understanding, of course, that no return is guaranteed)

Fund A has an expense ratio of 0.33%. After 10 years of earning an average annual 7%, the returns that were lost to fees equaled $637.53 or 6.6%.

Fund B has an expense ratio of 1.44%. After 10 years of earning an average annual 7%, the returns that were lost to fees equal a whopping $ 2,620.69 or 27.1%. That's a loss of almost 1/3 of your initial portfolio value over a 10-year period — just for fees! So you can see that these hidden fees are important and can be very costly to your portfolio.

Although we have only looked at mutual funds, they aren't the only culprits. You need to look "under the hood" for every asset in your portfolio. Annuities, especially variable annuities can be very confusing and costly. They are so especially problematic that they get their own chapter (**See Chapter 8**).

For individual stocks and bonds, there is the "bid and ask spread" that affects the fees paid. Most securities (stock and bonds) are transacted through exchanges (physical and electronic) with firms who "make a market" in that security. These market makers will maintain the market price for the securities they keep as inventory. The price will always include a bid and ask. For example, if you wanted to buy stock A with a bid of $10 and an ask of $11 you will pay $11 to buy it. Sellers would get only $10. The market maker keeps the spread. This is their cut for being the middleman and helping to maintain a market so you can readily buy and sell. The less demand there is for the security, the greater the spread.

Said another way, to have any transaction of individual securities (including ETFs), you need to have two parties — each getting something to their advantage (either the price they like or the security they want to buy/sell).

Many firms have been sanctioned by the regulatory agencies for shady market making, especially when some have been cited for pressuring their sales team to recommend stocks that they wanted to unload from their inventory. This created a blatant conflict of interest.

The key take-away here is that the best way to protect yourself and your estate from these hidden fees is to carefully and forensically evaluate all of your investments. Many fees are hidden in the small print of offering prospectuses. Enlisting the help of an advisor that understands investments and the law, can help you to identify and minimize the "leaks" that are depleting your estate, drop by drop.

8 – Variable Annuities: The Scourge of the Earth

Initially I wrestled with the word "scourge," pondering if it was too harsh. After really thinking it through, I concluded that scourge really is the best word choice. Here's why...

Annuities are investments issued by insurance companies. They come in three flavors, generally: fixed, indexed, and variable. The first two kinds are sold by individuals with an insurance license and have protections against loss of principal. The last, the variable annuity, is a product sold by someone with an insurance license plus a securities broker license. Regardless of which kind you get, annuities are contracts between the owner and the insurance company, much like a life insurance policy. But the similarity stops there.

The simplest explanation is that when you invest in an annuity any growth in your investment is tax-deferred until you start to withdraw. The sales pitch is that your annuity will be invested (more on that in a bit), and grow, tax-deferred until you decide to annuitize (or start to draw income from it based on a schedule you choose, such as — for life or 10 years certain, etc.).

However, if you withdraw any funds before age 59½ you will be subjected to an IRS penalty of 10% in addition to the ordinary income taxes. This is one reason why investors over age 59 are hot targets, since part of the sales pitch is that they can access their money anytime they want, without the IRS penalty. Sounds fantastic, right? If only it were that simple.

You can purchase annuities two different ways. You can make a single lump sum investment or invest over a period of time. You can start the annuity in deferred mode (grow for now, start income later) or immediate annuitizing (when you want your ordinary income payments to start immediately).

Despite how confusing variable annuities can be, they are sold and purchased in droves. The main reasons for this are fear and greed. Annuities, in general, pay sales reps some of the highest commissions available for investment products. Variable annuities, in particular, pay the highest out of all annuity commissions. Many firms will highly incentivize sales by offering sales reps exotic vacations and other bonuses on top of lucrative commissions. The fewer details and facts that are explained during client sales presentations, the easier these are to sell. Instead sales reps tend to emphasize issues that generate fear in retirees, especially the worry that they will outlive their nest egg.

Investors get caught up in the sales pitch that there is no limit to how much they can sock away and the icing is that all of their growth is tax-deferred, until they start making withdrawals. And it sounds ideal, yes? Well, not exactly. In fact, there are some serious concerns that investors need to know *before* they sign that annuity contract.

Regardless of the type of annuity, there are some common characteristics. One is that they often involve very strict withdrawal (liquidation or surrender) penalties. Even though someone over 59½ no longer has to pay an IRS penalty, they still could lose a big chunk of their investment to their withdrawal fees. Some annuities have a strict early penalty fee structure for 10 years or more. How else do you think they're paying for your advisor's trip to Monte Carlo or Bali?

Now onto the scourge — variable annuities. Variable annuities became a hot investment back in the late 1990s, when the stock market was hot and booming. The sales pitch was easy. You can sock away as much as you want and all of your growth would accumulate tax-deferred with no taxation until you started to withdraw. With a booming stock market, the idea of having large equity investments accumulating in a deferred account, sheltered from taxation, sounded like a dream. That is until the market did what it always does — correct and cycle down.

The stock market bubble burst of early 2000 created a new issue. What happens if there are no gains, just losses — that can't be deducted because they are in a tax deferred account? An estimated $5 trillion in asset value was lost. Any of that in deferred accounts could not be deducted for any tax saving benefits. The impact of a market crash isn't the only problem with variable annuities. There are several more reasons why variable annuities are in my assessment, the scourge of the earth.

Taxation:

One problem is the taxation selling point. The tax deferral on equity growth is actually a disadvantage, and one poorly explained by the sales rep. While taxes are deferred until you withdraw money, when you take that money out, you will be taxed at ordinary income tax rates. Those are the higher rates that apply to things like your salary, Social Security, or pensions. Imagine that!

You took investments, and wrapped them in an insurance policy, and then took that money and invested it in the stock market or other securities. If you had by-passed the insurance company and invested it directly, any gain would have been taxed at the long-term capital gains rates. The tax-rate for long-term capital gains (0%–15%) is much lower than ordinary income tax rates (0%–39.1%).

You will generally end up paying more taxes on the money when you pull it out of the variable annuity as ordinary income, than if you just paid the regular capital gains tax in a non-deferred investment.

Poor investment options:

Variable annuities generally offer few guarantees that assure you will at least get all of your principal back. The investment options are also quite limited and more difficult to assess than other mutual funds. There is also a diminished ability to be invested in the right securities at the right time. Investments in certain securities are mandated by the contract whether they are the best market option or not.

Bad for your estate:

One big advantage in the estate planning arsenal is the stepped-up basis at death. What this basically means is that if you buy an investment and it appreciates, when you leave that for your heirs, the current price becomes their new basis point, or cost basis for calculating future gains. They aren't assessed taxes on the gain that the asset has already experienced while you owned it. This is a huge tax planning benefit. However, gains like this in a variable annuity, do not receive this stepped up basis tax savings. Your cost basis is passed onto your heirs. So, when they take the money out (in lump sum or over time), they are responsible for all of the gains, which will be taxed at ordinary income rates…back from the date of original purchase.

Whereas, if you have invested directly in the market, any capital gains would have been erased at your death.

Fees, fees, fees:

I can't emphasize enough that no matter how "perfect" variable annuities sound during the sales pitch, they have *significant* drawbacks. I can assure you that during the sales presentation, the sales rep will be multiplying your available funds by about 7% to calculate *his* return on *your* investment. And his suitcases will be all packed for that bonus vacation he's getting too. Oh but 7% isn't what it will cost *you*…you're going to pay more.

If you want your money back early, expect to pay a lot more as the withdrawal (surrender) penalty. And if you stay invested, the expense ratios (remember we talked about this in **Chapter 7** on hidden fees) are among the highest of any mutual fund. It is not unusual to see annual deductions for fees that exceed 3% a year. Whether you keep it or dump it, you'll still be socked with a huge loss to fees.

I think this gives you some idea, of why I think variable annuities are the scourge of the earth. There are more reasons, but the ones I just outlined are some of the most egregious. Unfortunately, most of the variable annuities sold serve sales reps and the firms they represent more than the investors to whom they are sold.

9 – The Benefits of Having Someone Who is Always in Your Corner

One other item is at the core of having a successful "Make It Last" plan. It's who you have in your corner, and whether they are a "fiduciary."

Fiduciary duty, in a nutshell, means that someone is legally obligated to act in *your* best interest. Trust and confidence are the price of the ticket these advisors pay for going to your dance. A fiduciary must recommend, service, and advise in such a manner that your best interests are *always* served.

Some investors find the concept of fiduciary responsibility a bit confusing. Most people generally assume that an advisor of any sort has an ethical duty to advise with integrity and honesty. However, a fiduciary relationship is much more powerful and precise than any simple expectation of integrity.

Fiduciaries also bear the responsibility for preparing themselves to adequately serve *your* best interest. This includes being certain that:

- they possess the knowledge to advise you properly,

- they have awareness of any potential conflicts of interest that could interfere with their complete commitment to serve your needs,

- they have vision that allows them to anticipate issues that could influence their advice and enable adjustments to serve you more efficiently,

- they possess the experience to advise in the areas they represent and are committed to maintaining ongoing knowledge that could impact their qualifications,

- and above all, they must without compromise, advise you with the utmost of purpose to serve your needs, preserve your trust, and maintain your confidences.

The importance of fiduciary relationships is so critical that even the U.S. Department of Labor is taking action to expand and reinforce fiduciary responsibility. Despite much effort to hinder its passage, the Department of Labor is rolling out in 2016 a new fiduciary rule.

At the core of the new DOL Fiduciary Rule is the reform of the commission compensation that sales reps can receive for investments in retirement assets. More specifically it addresses the requirement for a fiduciary advisor relationship that protects consumers from conflicts of interest.

"Today, I'm calling on the Department of Labor to update the rules and requirements that retirement advisors put the best interests of their clients above their own financial interests. It's a very simple principle: You want to give financial advice, you've got to put your client's interests first."
– President Barack Obama, February 23, 2015

This new rule will require retirement asset advisors to adhere to a fiduciary standard, legally requiring them to serve their clients' best interests without conflicts. Of course, this creates a huge dilemma for the sales reps who planned to enjoy a bonus trip to the Bahamas, that investors paid for in commissions when they invested their IRA rollovers.

The financial industry is no doubt in transition. And many firms may scramble to evolve into fiduciary advisories.

One primary example of fiduciary duty is the attorney-client relationship. As an attorney, I already have a legal and ethical obligation to act in my legal client's best interest. Any recommendations I make must, above all, be examples of the highest standard of care. I could never make a recommendation that favored anyone over my client, including favoring myself. In other words, I am always in my client's corner, advocating what is best for them.

This fiduciary standard is a big deal for close relationships, where you are entrusting your well-being to the professional opinion of another. It would be natural for you to expect that this fiduciary standard extends to the financial and investment world. But, in a word, it doesn't.

And even if the retirement asset industry may soon be required to adhere to a fiduciary standard, this rule does not impact *non-retirement* assets and the advisors who might pursue your non-retirement investments.

Most "financial professionals" fall into the category of salesperson or agent. Is that "your" agent? No, they are the agent of their broker/dealer or of the insurance company. They are not obligated to watch out for your best interests. Not even close.

In fact, the most they are required to do is to make sure that the investment product — the thing they are selling you in exchange for a commission — is "suitable" for you. Not the best, just suitable. And it means, without question, that one of these sales people, who are still calling themselves your "financial advisor," can favor and recommend a product that pays them a higher commission — and favor it over the best product — just as long as the investment is suitable.

How about an another illustration?

Let's assume you need cataract surgery. You go to a medical office to discuss your vision issues. While you're there the licensed doctor recommends that instead of getting those cataracts fixed, you should have a face lift to get rid of all of those wrinkles you have (you got those from worrying if you will have enough money for the rest of your retirement years). Hey, after all, it's the latest hot idea. Who wouldn't want to look 20 years younger with no sign of wrinkles?

Now, recommending a face lift to someone with wrinkles may be "suitable" but the problem is, that isn't what you really need or what you came for. You still need those darn cataracts removed. You might look amazing without wrinkles, but your vision is too blurry to even see the fabulous new you. This is the difference between "suitable" and being legally obligated to recommend and service your best interests with fiduciary duty.

Now the next big question is usually, whether or not there are financial advisors who are like fiduciaries instead of commission sales reps, who will have **your** best interests, to guide any investment strategies and recommendations? There are!

The financial advisor fiduciary who keeps your best interests are called Investment Advisor Representatives, and they work at firms called Registered Investment Advisers, or RIAs.

A Registered Investment Adviser must be registered* with the SEC (Securities and Exchange Commission) or a state regulatory agency. RIAs have a formal fiduciary responsibility to their clients. They are fundamentally and legally obligated to provide advice that is appropriate for the client and always act in their client's best interest.

---

* **Registration refers only to the formal process of registering with a regulatory agency, and does not indicate or imply a certain level of skill or training.**

As an Investment Adviser Representative, this is a fiduciary role that I fulfill for many of my estate planning clients who then became my financial planning clients. In fact, this makes me a dual fiduciary. Not only am I legally obligated to provide the most appropriate legal advice to guide an estate, I am also legally obligated to only make investment recommendations that are in my clients' best interests.

This dual fiduciary experience is quite comforting for many families. Often for the first time, they really know what it is like to have someone who is always in their corner. They no longer worry that any "hot investment tip" is hot because the sales rep is earning a trip to the Bahamas for selling it. They now know that along with the trust and confidence of client-attorney privilege, they also can experience the same bond of trust that their financial well-being and best interests are the ONLY factors that matter.

I take great pride in this dual fiduciary role that I get to have in my clients' lives. As frustrated as I get whenever I discover that a client has been poorly advised in the past, I know that going forward, they have me in their corner. It helps to protect my clients from what happened to Paul and Diane. And as a dual fiduciary, I do everything possible to make sure that a client's estate is protected legally and financially to preserve their retirement well-being and to preserve their legacy wishes.

10 – The Essential Elements of a "Make It Last" Plan

So, you've made it this far into the book. Here's where it all ties together and where you develop a game plan for how to take control of your retirement and "Make It Last."

Let's review what we've covered so far. We have gone over:

- Assessing Net Worth

- Investment Strategy

- Long-Term Care Planning

- Income Taxes

- Types of Advisors & Proprietary Assets

- Limiting Hidden Fees

- Avoiding Variable Annuities

- Working with Fiduciary-Standard Advisors

Each of these topics has a direct connection to preserving your nest egg and making sure your journey through retirement is as smooth as possible.

When I evaluate a legal client's financial situation, I look for the Fab Five Essential Elements of a "Make It Last" plan.

1) Retirement Cash Flow Planning
Short–Term Liquidity
Guaranteed Income

2) Long-Term Care Plan
Spousal Protection Plan

3) Proactive Income Tax Planning

4) Investment Asset Make-up
Low Fee Investments
No Proprietary Assets
No Variable Annuities

5) Fiduciary-Standard Advisor

If you would like a handy checklist to see if you have the "Fab Five," look for one at the back of this book. And if you would like to print out another or share the checklist with a friend, go to www.makeitlastbook.com/tools and download it. Of course, if you really wanted to be a friend, you would recommend that they purchase their own copy of this book — it costs less than a decent haircut.

1-Retirement Cash Flow Planning

For this first element, you want to make sure that you completely understand your situation about what you own, what money you have coming in, and what money you'll need going out. I try to focus on making sure that clients have sufficient short-term liquidity so that they don't have to time the market, and sell assets to cover an immediate shortfall. That's my short-term bucket.

In addition, I want to see if the client has, or could benefit from, some form of guaranteed income. Too often, a client is just relying on social security, and spending down their assets out of an investment account. Depending on what they have to start with, we may be able to create a private "pension" that will give them guaranteed income for life.

2-Long-Term Care Plan with Spousal Protection

For this second element, I want to make sure that my clients have a plan in place to address the possibility that either one of them or both may need some type of assistive or nursing care. This goes beyond making sure there is a funding source for potential expenses, but includes planning to assure maximum asset preservation to qualify for maximum government benefits.

3-Proactive Income Tax Planning

For this third element, I want to make sure that my client is paying attention to their income taxes early in the year and planning around the applicable tax brackets. This work includes planning out IRA distributions (early if appropriate), and managing which investments (bonds vs. stocks) are held in which accounts (IRA vs. "taxable" investment accounts). Finally, I want to make sure that clients are considering what the income tax impact will be to their kids and beneficiaries and planning around that.

4-Investment Asset Make-Up

In this fourth element, I want to make sure clients have an investment portfolio that matches their risk tolerance, and includes only low-cost, low-fee investments. I want the asset make-up to exclude proprietary assets. Finally, I want to make sure that clients have avoided any variable annuities, or have a plan to get out of any they might already have as soon as possible.

5- Fiduciary-Standard Advisor

In this fifth, and final, element, I am looking to make sure that my client has a fiduciary-standard advisor. Many times clients are surprised to learn that their current advisor is just a salesperson. That includes most advisors working at the large wealth management companies that are the household names. I recommend that you work exclusively with an independent Registered Investment Advisory firm so that you get an advisor that is strictly working in your best interests.

You can check whether your advisor is an RIA by going onto http://brokercheck.finra.org. That site will let you enter information about your advisor, or the advisement firm.

On the results page, if you see only "Investment Adviser" below the name of the result, you know you've got someone working as an RIA. If you see "Broker" with "Investment Adviser", this is someone who can either be earning commissions on sales, or fees on investment or both. I recommend someone who just has "Investment Adviser" as a result.

From that site you can check on all kinds of information about the advisor. You can see how much in assets under management they have, as well as the mandatory disclosures they have to make

I think that these five elements are the bare minimum that clients should have in their financial lives. However, a comprehensive team will cover much more than this. This is how you can be sure to have a nest egg that really does last as long as you do, and beyond.

More Information About Private Client Capital Group

How we work with you: A process-driven, consultative approach

The personal relationship that we develop with each of our clients starts with an initial meeting to identify goals, objectives and risk tolerance levels. We gather your personal information and discuss your financial goals and concerns. We review our philosophy and investment approach with you so that you fully understand our portfolio management approach. You will complete a risk tolerance assessment that will become the basis for discussing the allocation of various asset classes within your portfolio.

Over the course of the next few meetings we will discuss retirement accumulation or distribution planning; evaluate educational funding needs; review your tax situation, and go over any other items we believe are critical to your financial success. If you own a closely held business, we may also discuss business succession planning strategies. We may run a financial projection to evaluate the feasibility of attaining your goals. With your permission, we will consult with your other advisors including CPAs.

Once you select an allocation, we will work on an implementation plan that will coordinate investment of your portfolio between qualified (tax-advantaged) assets and nonqualified assets in order to maximize tax efficiency.

Depending on the size of your portfolio and your preference, we may dollar-cost average your assets into the market over a period of up to six months.

Your assets are held at a reputable third-party custodian that will furnish you with monthly reports either online or via mail. Private Client will provide you with a quarterly performance report that will clearly show your performance, net of all fees, and compared to applicable market indexes. Our strategy includes enhanced rebalancing of your portfolio to make sure you don't veer from the allocation we have agreed upon. This ensures that your portfolio risk is consistent with your risk tolerance and financial goals.

We will meet with you periodically to discuss your financial situation and progress toward your goals. As your financial goals change, we can make adjustments to your strategy as needed.

Our Investment Philosophy

We have developed and refined a consistent, strategic investment philosophy supported by a significant body of academic research. We believe that a widely diversified portfolio of investments tailored to each client's unique risk tolerance level and financial goals is key to financial success.

A study conducted by an independent research firm found that the average return of the S&P 500 over the last 20 years was 9.9% per year, yet the average equity investor earned only 5.2%[*]. Why? Most individual investors gravitate toward the next "hot" investment and let emotions rule their portfolio.

The goal of our approach is to take the emotion out of investing in order to capture market returns while minimizing volatility.

If you would like more information about working with Victor J. Medina and Private Client Capital Group, you can visit **www.privateclientcapitalgroup.com** for more information.

Private Client Capital Group is registered as an investment advisor with the states of New Jersey and Pennsylvania, and only transacts business in states where it is properly registered, or where it is excluded or exempted from registration requirements.

---

[*] Source: 'Quantitative Analysis of Investor Behavior,'DALBAR, 2015; S&P data provided by Standard &Poor's Index Services Group, with results based on the S&P 500 Index. Indexes are not available for direct investment. Their performance does not reflect the expenses associated with the management of an actual portfolio. Past performance is not a guarantee of future results.

Registration does not constitute an endorsement of the firm nor does it indicate that the advisor has attained a particular level of skill or ability.

Before making an investment decision, please contact the office at 609-476-9269 to receive a copy of Private Client Capital Group's Form ADV Part 2A and the Private Client Advisory Agreement, both of which include Private Client's fee schedule. This information is intended to serve as a basis for further discussion with your professional advisors. Although great effort has been taken to provide accurate information and explanations, this information should not be relied upon for making investment decisions.

All investing involves risk, including the potential for loss of principal. There is no guarantee that any strategy will be successful.

About the Author

Victor J. Medina holds a distinct designation as a dual fiduciary for his clients. He is a practicing Estate Planning and Elder Care attorney, as well as an Investment Advisor Representative, assisting with asset protection, retirement and investment management, and proactive tax planning.

Victor is the founder of Medina Law Group, concentrating on estate planning, and the president of Private Client Capital Group, a registered investment advisory firm. He brings a family-centered approach with a focus on practical solutions for families and high-net worth individuals.

Victor is married to Jennifer Medina, a school psychologist, and they are the parents of three sons (Aidan, Lucas, and Dylan). He lives and practices in Pennington, NJ.

Glossary

Form 1099 – IRS form issued to report various types of income, other than wages, salaries and tips. This income can be from investments, sale of property, dividends, or interest income.

12b-1 fee – An annual marketing or distribution fee on a mutual fund. It generally between 0.25%-1% (maximum) of a fund's net assets.

401(k) – A form of qualified employer-sponsored defined contribution plan. Contributions may be made pre-tax or post-tax.

Agent – Individual who has been legally appointed to act on behalf of another person.

Annuity – A form of insurance or investment entitling the investor to a series of payments over a defined period (fixed years, or even lifetime).

Appreciation – Increase in the value of an asset.

Asset – Property owned by a person or company, generally regarded as having value and available to meet debts, commitments, or legacies.

Assisted living – Housing for seniors that provide nursing care, housekeeping, and prepared meals as needed.

Bond – A debt investment, where investors loan money in exchange for interest on their loan, for a set length of time.

Broker – Intermediary paid a commission for executing customer orders.

Buy-and-hold – Investment strategy where an investor buys selective investments and hold them for a long time with the investment philosophy that over the long-haul investment appreciate.

Capital gains – Increase in the value of a capital asset (investment or real estate). Capital gains can be short term (less than 1 year) or long-term (longer than 1 year) and must be claimed on income taxes.

Cash flow – Incomings and outgoings of cash.

Certificates of deposit – Promissory note issued by a bank.

Chronic illness rider – A form of accelerated benefits rider permitting access to a benefit under a defined chronic illness, like nursing home care or assisted living facility care.

Commission – Fee paid to an agent or broker in exchange for facilitating or completing a sale transaction.

Cost basis – The purchase price an investor pays for a security or asset, plus any out-of-pocket expenses or additional investments

Disability – Physical or mental condition that limits a person's ability to interact with his/her surroundings or other people.

Elder care planning – Planning focusing on the needs of seniors to help navigate the legal, financial, and medical landscape.

Equity – The value of shares issued by a company.

Estate administration – The process of transferring assets, filing taxes, and settling debts of a decedent.

Estate planning – The act of preparing for the transfer of a person's wealth and assets after death, and planning for incapacity.

Estate tax planning – Planning for the minimization of estate taxes (federal and state).

ETF – Exchange Traded Fund is a marketable security that tracks an index, a commodity, bonds or a basket of assets. Unlike a mutual fund, ETFs trade like stocks on a stock exchange.

Expense ratio – Annual fee that mutual funds or ETFs charge their shareholders.

Fiduciary – A person to whom property or power is entrusted to act in the best interest of another.

Financial planner – Any of a number of designation of investment professional assisting people meet financial goals.

Financial retirement planning – Financial planning focused on post-retirement distribution and legacy planning.

Fixed annuity – Insurance contract that makes fixed payments, or credits a fixed amount to an investor over time.

Fixed income – An income from a pension or investment that is set at a particular figure and does not vary or rise with the rate of inflation.

Fund manager – Employee that manages the investment of money on its behalf or that of an outside client.

Guaranteed death benefit – A benefit term that guarantees that the beneficiary, as named in the contract, will receive a death benefit if the annuitant dies before the annuity begins paying benefits.

Guardianship – Legal process where a person is appointed to manage the care and finances of an incapacitated person.

Health care directives – Legal document setting forth health care desires in terminal conditions or permanently unconscious states.

Heirs – Person inheriting assets from another.

Home health care – Long-term care provided in the home, typically by an aide.

Income rider – Insurance contract provision adding an attached benefit that solves for longevity risk by providing a lifetime income stream.

Indexed annuity – Type of annuity that grows based on the performance of an equity index.

Interest rate sensitivity – A measure of how much the prices of a fixed-income asset will fluctuate as a result of changes in the interest rate environment. Securities (bonds or stocks) that are more sensitivity will have greater price fluctuations than those with less sensitivity.

Traditional IRA – An individual retirement account (IRA) that allows individuals to direct pre-tax income towards investments that can grow tax-deferred. Tax is assessed when assets are removed at ordinary income tax rates.

IRA rollover – A type of individual retirement account into which employees can transfer assets from their former employer's retirement plan when they change jobs or retire.

Liens – Property right over an asset until a debt is discharged.

Long-term care insurance – Insurance coverage that provides nursing-home care, home health care, personal or adult day care for individuals above the age of 65 or with a chronic or disabling condition.

Medicaid – Joint federal and state entitled program that helps elderly people pay for long-term care.

Money market accounts – Non-financial account that pays interest based on current interest rates in the money markets.

Mutual funds – Investment program funded by shareholders that trades in diversified holdings and is professionally managed.

No-load mutual fund – Mutual fund in which shares are sold without a commission or sales charge.

Nursing home – Skilled nursing institution providing residential accommodations plus health care, typically for elderly people.

Ordinary interest – Category of income earned from interest, wages, rents, royalties, and other similar income.

Pension – Defined benefit where regular payments are made during retirement from an investment fund which the person or the employer, or both, have contributed during working time.

Portfolio – Bundle of investments of securities with expectation of a return.

Power of attorney – Legal document granting authority to act for another person in specific legal or financial matters.

Qualified dividends – Type of dividend to which capital gains tax rates are applies.

Registered investment advisor – Investment adviser registered with the Securities and Exchange Commission (SEC) or a state's regulatory agency.

Registered representative – Stockbroker, or account executive, who is licensed to sell securities for a commission.

Required minimum distribution – The minimum amount that the IRS requires must be withdrawn each year from all tax-advantaged retirement plans starting in the calendar year following the year in which the plan holder reaches age 70.5. Roth IRAs are exempt from this rule.

Return of premium – Insurance contract provision provide for a return of the premium invested without surrender charges, and minus any distributions previously made.

Risk tolerance – An investor's ability or willingness to accept declines in the prices or value of investments while waiting for them to increase in value.

Sequence of returns risk – The risk of receiving lower or negative returns early in a period when withdrawals are made from an individual's underlying investments.

Short pay premium – The payment of premiums on an annual basis for a period of time.

Single premium – The payment of premiums in a lump-sum.

Suitability – The tendency for an investment to be suitable for a client. Considered a lower standard of care than a "fiduciary" standard.

Underwriting – The process of evaluating the risk of insurance a person. Higher-risk individuals and assets will have to pay more in premiums to receive the same level of protection as a low-risk person.

Variable annuity – Insurance contract in which premiums are invested in a sub account in securities.

Volatility – Tendency for an investment to increase and decrease in price over a given period of time. Higher volatility will have bigger swings up and down over a shorter period of time.

Withdrawal (surrender) penalty – Fee levied on a life insurance or annuity contract upon the cancelation of the policy. The fee is used to cover the costs of keeping the insurance policy on the insurance company's books. Fees act as an economic incentive for investors to maintain their contract, and they allow insurance companies to have reasonable expectations for the frequency of early withdrawals.

Do You Have The Essential Elements Of A

PLAN?

❏ Retirement Cash Flow Plan
  Short Term Liquidity
  Guaranteed Income

❏ Long-Term Care Plan
  Spousal Protection Plan

❏ Proactive Income Tax Planning

❏ Investment Asset Make-up
  Low Cost/Fee Investments
  No Proprietary Assets
  No Variable Annuities

❏ Fiduciary-Standard Advisor